Dovecote

Heather Fuller

ESTRANGED FROM ITSELF
A BOOK
A DOVECOTE DEDICATION
TO THE AMERICAN COUSIN

with warm regards
for Michael
Heather Fuller
12.16.01

EDGE

Typography, Design, & Illustrations: Michael Rupertus
Cover Photography: Gerald Fuller
Cover Design: Kaia Sand

Heather Fuller is also the author of *perhaps this is a rescue fantasy*
(Edge, 1997).

The author thanks the editors of the following publications, in which versions
of poems in this collection previously appeared: *alyricmailer, Aufgabe, Big Allis,
Cartograffiti, Combo, The George Washington Review, Membrane, Philly Talks
Newsletter, Poetry New York, Pom², Primary Writing, The Tangent, tongue to boot,* and
Zazil. Some of the poems also appeared as a chapbook, *beggar,* published by
Situation Magazine; thanks to editors Mark Wallace and Joanne Molina.

Thanks to Buck Downs, Perreaoult Daniels, Susan Goldman, and Garrett
Kalleberg for multimedia motivation. Thanks to Rod for editorial advice
and many other gifts. And special thanks and love to Gray.

Edge Books are published by *Aerial* magazine.

Distributed by Small Press Distribution, Berkeley, CA.
1-800-869-7553
orders@spdbooks.org

ISBN: 1-890311-12-x

Edge Books
P.O. Box 25642
Washington DC 20007

aerialedge@aol.com

www.aerialedge.com

Dovecote

Dovecote

Go to http://www.ameritel.net/lusers/edzerne/artstdc.htm

Click Perreaoult Daniels

Then

Dear Perreaoult Daniels:

what is its hold on us

the shelter walls were the color of street is
celadon a color because the celadon walls or
was it a prehistory   to speak there means to
speak of the dead   we are now dead as we are
past tense
                                   Perreaoult
painted there Heather made poems there except
the wall is not there   was it to prove
technical expertise that resulted in portraiture
on the wall a veil sprouting horns my hair

Perreaoult   as if to ask of paintings
people ask after the dead not where are they now
but they were painting and making poems until
the wall shut them down they were crazy and
perhaps they would have been better off
somewhere except here we are shoveling
streets   the most commonly found object on
the side of streets is ladies' underwear this
I cannot explain tho' here are two witnesses
Gray and Rod will tell you

PD did you know the rules

if not celadon at least it smelled like dirt well
there were trenches   OK so I've never gone
hungry but I want out of the hunger contract

some will eat dirt and lie in trenches how did we
get the ink so dirt rotten it rankled in our pens
so we took to scratching the wall shaking down for dear

Perreaoult   did you recover the brush the pen

the person in the shelter will begin to identify with

brush	pen
soft texture	bed
warm color	companion
piece of string	line to the stomach
silkscreen	place been there before

or the dots gather to one relentless thing

Dear Perreaoult Daniels:

spitting out treacherous words

bodies filled with glass   as if glass-blown
interiors so we might break but not show
1400 shelter people   some said they were there
on purpose   I had no purpose but standing up
right and not bumping slipping to break in
trenches you'll take your vision
ary out

PD   there are you living by the city or
living by the ocean

Jesse asks Heather how is Perreaoult   Jesse's
skeptical because Jesse's the only one not dead
so everything Heather says is an enormous
grain of salt   he was a good artist that Perreaoult

then I know he is dead   as the living is
the convergence of how we got there

                    stopping the endless argument

or involuntary instituting stopping living against
the wall

PD   I lived there charmed

the last painting there was the color of pins and
needles and sometimes the artists disappeared
therefore would be dead   like speaking in
past tense assuming the subject is dead too polite
to speak over the dead at present

then the dead would return and there'd be near
disappointment

sorry

I was just in the other room   Perreaoult what are
they doing there 1400 against the wall 1400 rules (#1)
when handling glass

Dear Perreaoult   did we have idle hands

not institutions we are living tho' there
we're dead   what we do to walls will be
our ruins   I don't remember how I got there
breaking 144-yr old law wandering abroad
in the street   Gray says every bit of
anger's a piece of clothing coming off

a Gun & Doll Show sort of shelter

where the dogs gone wrong
are let in the train flash of
the northeast city and women
coming from the south and
undressing there it is
the law

fayre and smouldering

that the bus driver decided
who would get off when
a contagion in the public
suitcase and a cord of tinder
sent 400 miles to be sent back
unclaimed wallowing in
the petrol failure of
don't count on it

colluding with job description
as the letter carrier a dust devil
who keeps coming back to
the same stalk of corn August
after August and a child
is found there

the dust devil arriving and
departing in the local consciousness
the dust devil timetabling a town
a weather postcard or
village imprint

*

pardonable the TV weather
when the corn stands tall

the old farmer the butt of
hi-jinx when the dust devil
deposits a child and takes
a reaper across the line

the farmer who is also a Fuller

a fuller being an occupation:
who beats or presses wool to make it fuller

the fuller for the recent part of
last century obsolete

fuller also a brand of beer
and a brand of brushes

this is where the oral history deadstop
for who is a fuller

*

blythe in the penny candy

what did we know of the *terroir*

kicking butt and growing to be
barkeep everything in fast fwd
it was but a spot of gout in
the camaraderie of old drunks who
were also teachers giving
the farms kids a classic
education shall we gather by
the loiter

there was this woman from WV
I won't give the town
but her name was let me go
in the day strangled by missing
garden hose a fugue perpetual
but slipping in the drunk day
garden missing a hose

who gets airlifted from the town
more south pole than
the south pole the town
wild chirpy malingering and
not straight up so things go missing

but nowhere where anybody
gets airlifted

*

waiting for the botulism in
the northeast city as every place
not coded south a pox
a taint on the scrapbook of
last resort and where Cornbread
took ill and found
the southern god

legendary the affliction in
Cornbread who would have not
if not for in the homecoming
laid on hands and
smote by tongues
his body reliquary factory

talking to dogs and
hearing dogs deep
listening to dogs
who don't find themselves
paid off and obsolete
only carney tragic in
any city Cornbread
punched out
his dancecard and
preached to dogs

*

hard to take

for anyone borne by
a dust devil and
smote by tongues
the innoculation
candy of the coded
dead lurker the burglar
robbing houses while
folks are in church
happy dancing
the old dances

droll and out of humour

when the job is
drunk and not wool or
dirt turned over and
turned over by
the fuller hitching north
blight as occupation

there was this woman caught
the bus coded south and
arrived in the local
consciousness a dust
devil deposit a postcard deadstop

Blood Program

we don't go there anymore pentecostal
with the mill kids but still the hazard
under the wine tree blotto slaven and scuppernong
lacuna in the thing that caught up and dragged in
the southern last capitol of narrative

where nobody's brother would wind
down and go to pasture go or reckon

and beaten for going with the mill kids in
Central Armature we heard nothing
and the talk of the deaf son and copped a heel

then a punctured eye

through Central arm in arm with
the compulsion to pick up the left
behind or watch the pilotlight in the wine

around the same time
a man dead in a shipment of bananas
and also his bag of clothes and hard tack there

glomming in the yonder there was suspicion
on our sides as we were beaten and in the wine and
what arm through the window

it wasn't fun when someone poked an eye purple
round your heart gobetween

and glomming in higher power
transference technique picking up the left
behind deaf son and not forgiving *you're*
notorious when you're poor

in the mill church stricken
sick for days we were

above the ravine after 8 yrs swept
away the tent city as if children
hadn't been grown there

when elsewhere NY drama getting fat
and educated and the bananas
shipping as if a higher power

and by the mill underwear showing
everywhere *we're sure someone poked
an eye* and copping a heel

elsewhere NY drama rock stars in
holiday home videos making
toasters desirable

until beaten like nobody's brother
back to wine and copping

in the ravine shoes lasted a lifetime
reheeling and reheeling we couldn't
imagine how worn down a heel
until the mill kids when our hands
went perpetually to our eyes
glomming

in the purple eye night watch

is god resting beside you
the panting you hear

the thirst that bit you
glomming in the wine and not
registering the dangling eye the
glomming transferability in well
heeled mill kids dabbling in
eye water

fifths down throat after throat
drowning old scratch why the ravine
was bursting and we glomming in
the hobo museum of our minds marveling

what fashioned from railyard tin a bouquet of
afflictions a hound the naked eye can't see

then the reverend Turnipseed

at the end of the day
soap ends for the poor people
gathering by the river

beside the sick feeling carefulness of
wet umbrellas while the dead man pulled from
the bananas and the only doctor an eye doctor

a birdbath full of vomit and then
the wine scabbing over a one-eyed
cicero at a busstopfull *don't get off at
this stop on the way home just don't
do it you*

hoarse on the bus as we'd caught it
from the mill kids leaving
for the merchant marine and we
getting fat and educated

abrahaming a way out of Central *bad
ticker* to get fat and in the wine

and at the end of the day
I can't tell you more
than people move on

Crandals Champion

Crandals Champeen
is a type of barbed wire and
I am eat up with bloodshed
of country road entanglements
on the wine train of brothers

the misunderstanding of the day
was a broke shovel on the quarter house

he opened the door and the devil just walked in

pulled from the carmine dirt
where Larry busted and Ice
stashed a knot of Jacksons

the hands have no feeling in public
so to the house a girl named after
religion retching parlance of
a lead chip lazy susan

I will be glad for no one speaking
in one place at one time until
the canker passes a child
reveals a sign

C. A. Hodge Spur Rowel

Hodge Spur along the Egypt Road
the work-release are passing
don't laugh sneeze or say
money in sight of church

that's what is said there I'm
not one to trifle when work is no
release

lie down with dogs to draw the sickness out

Peanut said better to die
jumping the fence than live
in the dirt on your belly

I'm not one to trifle

ash worn on the head
mistaken for conspiracy but
funny to be self-conscious

fallen in the dirt

H. Reynold Necktie

Reynold Necktie shut down
the tungsten mine for now but
not for children playing

the house cut into quarters
couldn't hold whole children

the floor supposed wood
turned out to be cement
for the tripped conductor of the wine train

snake skins packed into the split head
and a sermon rappelling through
the quarter

pull a chair up to the quarry
for the dragging of the pond

Stubbe Plate

Virginia tore through Plate
when a child could die
out of pain and Kelly Jo
unborn was a mouthful of dirt
devil to Doc's twister

flesh caught on a barb
was a good question

and spooked the quarter
children into meanness
against the street lamp gypsy
I'm not one to trifle

outrun by the wine train
Favorite Cousin went under

for what is said there
before drowning
the water tastes sweet

Brinkerhoff-Martelle Ribbon

Martelle Ribbon bit the American
cousin with kitchen familiarity
when scars took on a life of their own

the hands lose themselves in crowds

down by the devil's tramping ground
I'm not one to trifle with the work-release
in training for lifetimes of looking satisfied

the quarter house is a quarter empty

a pony of wine to wash the blood

when the sheriff came round
the back of the broke shovel
fit the knot on every head in town

follow the woman without shoelaces

this time every morning
working the pocket theater

I asked to accompany grief because
nothing has prepared her

working by the courthouse I can't
tell the children to go to camp

I have to go to work and the duplicator frenzy

how heavy my lids in the room's wasted light!

the children are acting out a commercial
they look like small fathers

again
the sleepworn shirt gives me away

when we turned away from
the children to look at traffic

because prime time and tendency to panic

follow the pregnant woman who walked from Helena to Richmond
via Savannah a grifter by her side

I heard he was a provider despite the penitentiary

there were no small scams yet no upset neighbors

and she posed as a boy as long as she could

birthweights are up in this cornfed town

it took a mappamundi like her

we learned next door a wad of cash
a gun laid out on the table

don't tell me about *the homeless odyssey*

the drifter who kept beating the boy
knew he was mistaken

follow the man who carries his personal
effects in a 9" x 12" ziploc

we learned not to upset our neighbor

I work in what was the banking ghetto

after four days on the job the many
ways and occasions to hang the flag

follow him
he returned from the institution with a lisp

he said it was a good place

good place for a letter bomb

I sent vitamins and postcards

working in the vatican of accountability

cash comes into my hands and I
find excuses

eventually the eviction of squatters
after the effigy of flags

it's easier to cry for the anonymous
neighborhood burning down

an action in missing

on the emergency room list of
unclaimed wallets and infants

in the street theater of cruelty
making Paris less a study

follow the beggar who claimed I had no shadow

tho' I'm taller since the risk capitol

growth spurt at 21!

listing sudden death as a potential
adverse side effect

where I work the buildings are salvageable

she's found places to sleep

stricken [from]

::record::

a teacher ::record:: helps a boy get a gun

it's about not ::record:: looking mistakable

::record::

houndstooth

accordion attache

bounty hunter provisions

::record:: I told the teacher about Pietro's

I was angry with the police again

I was mixed up in campaign finance reform

I was sweet shiftless and poor

and stricken

::record:: a boy is loaded

*

American Express makes it ::record:: *better*

"providing alternatives to jail
for persons who pose no
danger to the community"

Loan Consolidators for your ::record:: *problems*

> "but use purpose area #15A
> if primary focus is drug testing or
> purpose area #20 if focus is
> reducing jail crowding"

Effective Sanctions that Fit the ::record:: *Budget*

somehow I was caught up in this

and questioned about a family
::record:: resemblance

so early in the morning
::record::
the suspicious handbag on the sidewalk

the police are there
but I've neglected them

::record::

I've been told it's the Decade of the Brain

I must step aside

because the opera construction

there's a public fund for demolition

::record:: if you can find it

*

how did the smallest children ::record:: capture
the 4' wingspan   lash it to a branch
so the sewer birds ::record::

38

how did the smallest children
::record::
and unchecked pestilence

I am asking because there's a question
hanged

in America
::record::
the curiosity
of the fully-covered body

in America
[   ]
[   ]
of humility

one yr later we don't know
what happened on the ::record:: plane

how he ::record:: got the gun

Note: The performer of this piece may wish to engage a variety of tools to acti-
vate the embedded 2nd voice that speaks the ::record:: interruptions/refrain and
the bracketed spaces. Pre-recorded voice-overs and the timed emissions of "Talk-
Boy" novelty items found in your local Toys-R-Us are charming possibilities.

the room is every pocket door
and a long-haired red-headed woman

was where they took her
where they take every despondent Tennessee woman

I demanded to go to court

but where they take
housed in the consolidated freak show

and calling her The Inspector

I missed her

because the pocket door

in the docket a thumbnail
sketch out of time

the obsession almost certainly stemmed
from a desire to make something to
counteract the whole idea of "ending"

denying she ever was the Inspector

that what she did with what she found
in the sullen 8' x 12' was

      useless   *non-productive*

that she did despite the daily
mandatory destruction of hospital art
policy

despite the institution junk-bonding itself
where they took her

knowing I missed her
I wooed the myth of the 28-yr old Baltimore Glassman

I periodically disappeared for days
with memory of what I hadn't done

for each plea bargain
a Giacometti bride

who saw her slip into

what gravity of open coils

she may slip into narrative

if the template of every madman
could be so concrete

there in the D.C. street a template

there where Mr. Toynbee burned out
his car with him in it

how he knows to sit there every morning now
in the very spot when no one's told him nothing

what personal meaning when it slips

what I hadn't done was
hire the Dept of Ag

to slaughter the geese in the yards
like the rich hired

they were shitting in the car port

the geese

relocating the goslings
after surviving the rich

was somebody's job

I demanded a hearing

where the pocket door of law

who knew their rights
there in the yards

installing the Baltimore Glassman
in benefactor's quarters

in another institution

where there was first aid
but no Inspector

for every tax incentive
the geese or the Glassman

the door or the pocket

every article slipping

I missed on Rhode Island Avenue
the burned out chain of cars

and missing her it was useless

throwing the book where it ended

Press-On Stars w/ Instructions

but because I myself am afraid of
in the leisurely night
dog choked on Sirius   Orion
child-leashed in unkempt malls
where the satellite probation office

shopping is a one-hoodlum job
and I had said I hated
the clerks there who watched
migrant workers but not me so
there it is that I have hated

then Gray finds the dirty
constellations and somehow
laughing for days at
the porn price-check

but it was just martial arts
porn and everyone at ease I
again am eating crow in
the Pegasus night coughing up
Cassiopeia dreaming I told Rod
the Italian word for *lápiz*
then the highbeams die

in a park I thought named after Yeats
but it was another Irish province and I
walking the big walk big
waste of human composure and I
again am eating crow

because Gray keeps me
one foot on the ground I
have stopped entering traffic in
my love engine the damnedest
things empty into the street

from here we visit
the unappraised instrument in
a shop of innocents and pay out
rent to squirrels occasionally

ample laughers we are
giftgivers among token rodents
and looking up in the winsome
parse of heaven

I said I am liking this
country living hale setting off
car alarms not knowing
the hellbent kickstand in
for drugs and modems
the persistent state of
having to be apologized for

despite the unfazed clerks
on-behalf-of enters the mall
where I'm in eternal exit

Leo   Libra   I hate to
see you go and there
what my sisters call
virile night

in the germ terror
very spacesuit and poly this
all over dented cargo skin
I woke because the shark
outside *I'll be back man*
then stole away

in the decade I made out and off
grinding gears and lovers to
leave the Oz monkey decade
base and unbandaged and I
said terminal this

then Smitty spoke
a chorus of doors slamming
across the country and
the sextant lost its cool

from the decade the dead slipped out
and Jihad and Jewell held on
to shoulders and stable rayguns
then bottles leaked and
couldn't avoid closure

I'm going to the 80's
select a uniform
chemical bath
or victory garden

and not New York
where I've no truck
the beggar stalls where
the ratio of birds to
razor wire and D.C.'s
one blonde mother

I'm going there are
decisions to make and no one
will tell what anybody has so
here we are in the decade
erasing targets from our bodies
and swarms of fairy stories

the boy on the corner is losing
his pants that's fashion and I
should enjoy the lyric moment
yet the concept of filling
warheads with active tense
somehow seems a grammar past
due in sick anagrams

in the decade I didn't go
off and kept the electric slide
clean so don't sweat me

poets on porches

Power Lunch

if in the very love language I take
down to annotate the arbitrary
date I do not know until it
presents itself forced behind
the blondeheaded engine of poets &
poets since I left the wigged and
pawned mortar-gifted street
I'm no longer annoyed

because no city is elegant
the every conversation inelegant
legs and legs and laundry issues
tho' Buck & I stand mystified in
Downtown Bidness Improvement Districts

not party to part of
voting or improving one
strategy is to change
your number another to
slap it on a billboard but
I've lost track of where
my dues are going
where are they going

for arguments sake
trains ride less elegant
and every boutonniered rider less
elegant since the trains
fill up with 1/4 who left
the city the people left
are mad at those who left and
there's some explaining left

she was not mad at all
she made believe

the woman in love with the Kaiser
was not mad at all she
made believe I believe
the people get to the bottom
and work a mutually-agreed
subsidy do nothing but do it
well so I will take this lunch
roll heads later & see if Doug's around
to lay it down about late capital

beggar

no one will ask us to choose art or life – this is why we
understand large absences – I use the glass in front of
the painting to check my lipstick – rules bend themselves –
the reason why men carry rifles on public transport and I
use calendars less and less – to know the day by not a box
but what springs up – outside the gallery the beggar
almost looked in conversation with the two bourgeois –
wanted a light but got pocketsfull of mutter – a museum
is a cadaver of curious facts – but was he propped on crutch
or soldering iron – something lost in my spatial relations –
can I come without crying

that into the blurry – into the archetypal rest areas
of survivor women – that all is deft collection – pardon
me but are you taking that for depression or for depression –
vox polis of the carpark – fucked up scarecrow on a sugar
high – into the homeopathic pathology of personahood –
the beggar banned the mirror from public – into the security
guard – thought to get ahead of me didn't think I'd just
keep going – someone's notion of security drove her
to get ahead – into the man disrobing – the public grooming –
on borrowed fuel

on the proving ground in the month of the knuckle -- no sign
of a Good Woman nearby -- wrapped around the third row of
bricks nothing for the tent of fools -- what did I do with the $40
you gave me when you were alive -- when the dioxin work --
when the seeping into was the worker's compensation -- winded
beside the tracks -- who's stopping for the beggar in the orange hat --
20 signs and none will stop you -- whose language drops from
bridges and boxcars -- who became the choosers

bookplate

D.C. Impounding

Revival Center and
Shoe Repair

People Love People
House of Worship

Word Movers

D.C. General Baby A

[exhibit]

Baby Boy Morales
Baby Girl Luther 1
Baby Girl Luther 2
Potomac Baby C

[h it]
[hi]
[ex it]
[it]

lease

what does living here
mean for my shoes

deduct the lift
operator   thrift shop
consultant   jeweler to
the stars   and I am walking
in the most common
of drug store commandos

I must walk easier but
the cross walk

walking like buying

what buying one book for a school
does for the revolution what
your fisted jaw does for streetball

finding the way by the sweatlodges
when the woman starts eating again

some expression of piece-together

public

if you have access
to good libraries

read every page without pictures

don't ask what among the ruined
skin what hero in hero
-ine

look for places marked
by the dark brown sun

for the women storing web pages
from librarian to

don't nod doze or reshelve the fiche

dear patron
lose track midway

what head split from so much theft
that the bag on my shoulder

when dispensing aspirin amovement
she was stalking bread ends

because the exchange rate
travelers checks excepted

where sickness sits at the table
roachbaited

it is conference call logic
the way feet become part of the filth

febrile cargo for the bookfakir

followed from the train putting words together

she ran hard headon persistent traveler

to misery in high places

103 degree peril center

to the yellow journal or

the mercy fuck

prophecy

one day only madmen will entertain your children on the train maniacal
peekaboo and the woman looked eighthanded no
eight hands on her body on the train but I turned and she was in
the train holding the pole   no hands

please don't turn off porchlights to the trick-or-treat because you don't
believe

and one trick-or-treater missing

[in an all-time low act of organized idiocy
who leaves his patrol to search the gym

the FBI raids the shelter
trick or treating

                                        what cartel there

                              I didn't ask for a hand]

public

you have a fun life Etienne

drunk and the pepper spray

they were talking about how close the drive-by
killer because he had no name

Beware–Danger: American Dream #4

roll by the apt. complex and see who's shirtless

what makes the alley Historic
and the paternoster obliging

ride the bus for the man whose pyjama top

exhibitionism is not enough for him
lonely TV people the fear and love

his halfmast cover
story for the woman border

three-point turn and shudder

rent

bitumen pupil conspiracy
mummy epoxy

       [on loan]
       [iona]

we who will not be forgiven

to seize each 1-800 Mary
women exiting corporations

where Cerberus phone etiquette

all these women I should know
beneath the pentagon

so stay behind the cappuccino machine

each specialized work station

each longing compartment

public

shutterdizzy   cocksure
in the chemicals *au poivre*

the road one long pressure plate
the camera bloody with shots

in the long awaited specter of solidarity
when the lady returns from Space

inner ear working again
lovely skeleton keys

like a cyclist who's had a lot of wrecks
in the Escalator Improvement Program

or bus shelter mechanic
lost in the physical plant

it makes sense they left their stations
to stare at the eclipse

hire a jackhammer
pledge today in the roundabout debacle

no sidewalk has made a difference
made people stop talking to themselves

in the broken windows theory – theory of houses – I dwelled
meeting the disco visionaries and cop pastoral in the very
that passes for theory – a man still has to gather his prescription
drugs scattered on the bus floor alone – and busted for uppers
pink dreams on the K-9 wagon where what passes for funk I've
been know to fashion a disaster – knowing at least 30 seconals
of hipness – mistaking telegenic candidates for strange police
factions – PSAs for broken windows – and women outpacing
men in semiautomatic sales – an increase in decreases in subsets
of wounded and the sunburned cereal box resumes its steroid story –
when all along the cosmonauts were getting away losing track of
control locus – of commodities larger than credit rating in the sugar
water cold war left out for pests – the TV hr stretched into a decade
I don't have a typical day to take down the bad guy – some do
the job themselves – they gorge – drown

woman perpendicular to the man where the cop
and slow motorists here the cop will charge
child in a razed house

the friend going blind
and testifying Elder appear in white robes
I know I never told that I know never that
but now I'm telling

when the prodding to admission the heat
Elder and photo op young body young hand bleeding
codes I wanted to break but the able bodied
kindling

do not demolish where
someone once made money there or conspired
the friend going blind whose photo op for
Time dog & pony

I have need
for nothing   I eat C rations sometimes local food
the book is a bony land mark child in
jail diversion program except
the conviction and razed house stone's
throw to slow motorists

my job is to
clean up after attacks in daylight guarded
by children Marines I have need for
nothing on the ingratiation superhighway
three hot meals and able bodied
kindling a mission

storming the house
some sort of code working the penthouse lift
Elder in the mission was there a net for falling
workers   the poor are the church lacing
the machine and misery engineers where
the child

             in a snowjob or jail diversion
sex gets hard in the penthouse lift I'm not
bone tired I'm driving slow motorist but the dog
digging on the roof where a dog once jumped
a history of this and the friend going blind

                                        razing
dog & pony archive the Elder turning in church in
white robes seeing Gandhi there

                                the young girl
in jail diversion her job to carry cement for another 16 yr old
a bricklayer her job for C rations and I cleaning up
in the local cashbox

                        a net for falling workers
when the child entangled slow motorists while
the house razing woman breaking from the man so
prodding to admission when the heat or

                                cop diversion
most you can decipher from the news
but I have some time now and will try to
tell you the book is bone tired for the friend
going blind a snowjob alibi for the child
elsewhere when razing was called for questions
tho' got off Elder getting to know Gandhi

                                        there
a sighting in a creekbed from batoutofhell train child
the mind will play tricks tho' there's no history of
this and the young codes

                        I have need for

Birdman tells us nothing and I have nothing for the birds today
no meningitis scare or spinal tap

Birdman and a c ncentr c
circ e following I saw nothing in the br s d and v cant I'm not
going there ag in   .

lying in a cr ss walk lying so lights hit
only s c nds b fore but Birdman will not budge and I'm not talking to
the c ps was that me t lk ng to the c p

you will have your day
in c
  rt and I will have my spinal tap look Birdman has the rhinov r s and
the
Civ Dis unit has new spl tt r gu rds and I'm not going I'm not going
l mp because our day is dead our day is dead

n b dy
go l mp for you will have your day and Birdman will not
last a day I don't claim it was me told the c p and the meningitis
scaring the CD unit a Civ Dis n t in the wr ng location here is
Birdman going l mp this was no pr t st no demo no ex rc se of
rights you are in the wr ng location the wr ng location

did I
say that to the c p and no d fens no c rt app nted n thing or no
sh wd n Birdman is not lasting wants to get back to the birds and
I have n thing for him today no br s s und ng no spl tt r gu rd
day in c

rt as the Civ Dis n t looks a sad pack of children how
the cr wd c ntr l und ng could be its und ng tho' Birdman is neither
scary nor scared lying l mp in the c rc e of sad children I know
only what I pieced what I pieced Birdman has the rhinov r s this was
no ex rc se or p cn c

Birdman now back to the birds and I'm not
going there ag in in a sh wd n following c ncentr c circ e and rhino
v r s no meningitis

The Hopper Cult

herein the hotel house
we have this Restless Disease
and neither inevitable nor fortunate

this was my house
but not the bad fashion

I suppose my breast was convenient
when we translate the small language
of infants and pets

how we know break-in from lock-out

prophecy doesn't have to marquee
itself but the woman plucking
every browhair eyelash

How does Anna get cold germs?

mind is the bodysoup

why it took 3 police to pick
the guitarist off the construction site nextdoor

the reasons for rescheduling demolition!
why it is sexy to be confused

Che Hopper

Rod   in my visions *Motorcycle Diaries* became the runaway
bestseller and you toured the country as spokesperson for Verso

the trick was either to make noises or to finish sentences
for audiences overrating conjugation and splitting infinitives

resulting in sales far surpassing *God on a Harley*
(a spiritual journey)

Painterly Hopper

walking in all that city
eyethread detached
exhaust begins to smell like spumoni
and the odyssey ends in heroin
-ism

it's not like this in the paintings
until the way we look at each other
looks like the movies

one up on the figurative police
splicing sirens into dogs
riled in the pastel neighborhood
where batteries are never charged

if the Golden Mean
if all you need is
compass
ruler
piece of string
lifelong dislike of the figure

send fast
my walking I.D.
the charity of church people

Hopper Meteorology

lose the day of losses in
the I.D.
wrist watch
tape recording wo/ sound
poetics of the unsigned poem
the girl who enters rooms only to turn
around

a sort of dis
ease
and the many whose deficit chatter en-
idles

that snow in April would also seem a losing

or seeing through a wounded eye

broken down along the highway

luggage on a greedy median

tho' wrested here

Hopper in Horse Country

where does it end where does it begin
where howling cats are put out to pasture

where the Parking Meter Graveyard

in this country I have this fear
of losing my signature except
the men in the shelter
scraped off their fingerprints with butter knives

I signed the airmail declaration form
a letter bomber's not crazy enough

I am not from Little Rock
this is not my tractor

I who am caught by the eye

and the added confusion of Rosabud Magdalena

my résumé brays

who drives the pace car for wide loads
who follows or steers clear

don't look now but
it's the Freeway Incident Response Team

the man at the Greyhound sews a button on his coat
for 12 hrs straight

birds don't fly away because we're window dressing

people are dying in dayrooms with artists and Xmas trees

the horse is incidental

for who's keeping count

what I don't know about the civil war I will write about the civil war

Gray says it's dark like the 80's
a rogue front
diamond backs
beside of saints

Victoria ran
dear child
let the draft card burners come here &
teach the ten commandments

don't have the stomach for it
perfect prayer

enter magenta
genealogy on fire
child calling white *snow*
dying woman dreaming I am knocking on her door

lovely virago
in hysteria theater

we wanted to make bedshake

we exploded tent of fools

Victoria
all our deprivation chambers
are immunity failures
enunciations

indices pushed through our skulls

60 cords of letters
burning in the field

3rd degree
temper medicine
salvage wafer

misjudged
many women
yearning there

Victoria are we talking
a good game

stop me dead
4 days on base
medals for my canteen
my shrunken ration
stump of sickness
lost the tight gift
parceling
out of weight and soldiers

   trooper

coins scatter
opiate palm

after solitary trumped
the addictive
linen sleeve and turpentine
a single incision
left shrapnel
tuning in the ear

how the body compensates for fit

slow bodies of ether
pained with thinness/sloth

what textbook drawn
from the most rote testimony

the poet dropping in the field

as that's how it's done

lookoveryourshoulderl
ookoveryourshoulderlo
okoveryourshoulderloo
koveryourshoulderlook

the point   we cannot tell what
has been remembered from
what   reconstructed

tenants mourning [reconstructed]
Victoria California
5th woman in
botched line
derailing the way
she broke
the bottle tree
cobalt in the orange
choke of earth

1874
fretting boarders

liquor or urine in the well

long walk into town
if the woman could cast
out long walk if the woman could out
                                        last

my shouting preachers
half a ritual

the items taken from the casket
before the burial

half a ritual

crushing

what was left behind

for the record syn

        drome

a neutral convener
un founder

un hand her

skirt

        trailing

pitched a tent of fools

caul

the childrens replay
setting the house on fire
the house that is not set
but setting still
as they say down
the Gospel Road smoking
stalks of old growth put
that in your pipe and be
gone with you

you must have answered
me in your head

to be so caught up in the how-to
manual of visual support for
corporate litigation when
James recognized Carolina
as the visionary mecca
and bailed out of Virginia

touched 48 states in 33 days
on 52 dollars then caught in
Florida trying to ride a bicycle
to Italy where each house has
6 TVs 2 sometimes 3 on
all the time

I was born with the caul
but no guarantee

in the chorus line of you
have no talent and will be
asked to leave come quick
in 15 minutes I won't be able
to help you

that we'd had enough
and talked enough
fed the kids enough

where Gray says all that's left
for men is work

pooled consciousness of
courier or commuter

grandchildrens wither in my gut

why a lunch bag on a train
makes a mother teary

within 24 hrs the bitch will eat her pups

in the nostalgia for poverty
the birth cord and suckling

freed for no shred of evidence

a man in London has employed
12 workers to grind 7006
of his personal effects to pebbles
suitable for burial

in the future of course
I will consume again

word for first milk from the Latin

beestings
colostrum
green milk

the mother shuttling from
shelter to the bus on blocks in the junk
yard to stay under radar

so far
the books
car
LPs
art
and his father's sheepskin coat
ground down

shook loose the works in her arm

had a taste for something sweet

sugar tit
or other dirty bidness

she who goes back therein
a family of boxes is liable
to go Cartesian A B
to be around to save the kin
she is around as if she will stick
around as long as saving
is a magic bullet in the myth
of staying the magic bullet in
the likelihood of a stereopticon
on hand

                   therein
saving a gene for blank
faces spread out across the pool
a gene for the American
cousin for saving the kin a book
estranged from itself a dovecote
dedication to the American
cousin she is liable

                       to go
back there to stick around
crustacean tensile as long
as the myth of magic and
the likelihood of bullet she
is saving electrocution barrette
she is around to save the faces
the railroad messkit of a heart
with a plastic valve

pony ride

abandon
takes off its shirt

and the boy caterwauling there

it's not that we weren't reckless we
just kept it to the house
and the drunken shave basin
walloped in the southern eye of god

there the boy falls seamlessly
and again

gutter test to catch tripleweight or
hell

then the tailless squirrel jimmy
crack in Birdman's hand

I too was a boy so
don't tell
if the cops suddenly

but the boy landing as if
flippers there

or landing in the gutter and
coming to

or landing in the gutter
and going to
drinking and again
shirtless going

the way of acreage and pests or

solaria

we wouldn't have known where to
go in the wrecked latter-day ark
built by fools

so the boy caterwauling

proceed to nearest exits

in the pre-fab ark of one condition

I wager you'll be gone by cock's crow

and we said *brother*

this is for your poetry

doped to senses

here is my SSN
--- -- ----

I'm going to hi   on Am
airl n s
I may not make it

on the vacant phone line
when the cops

in absence of a flag
a shirt suffices

judge the enemy's distance
before raising

no time now
to act gingerly

Notes

p. 17   Combination gun & doll shows really do exist.

p. 21   Cant, the rap of the underworld, shows up in a few poems in this book. For example, a dead lurker, as the poem says, is a burglar who robs houses while folks are in church. Yellow peril isn't in the poem, but it's such a great phrase. It means prison grub.

p. 25   Eye water is gin.

p. 26   An eye doctor holds you in his/her gaze while stealing you blind. A cicero is a lookout person. To abraham is to fake sickness.

pp. 37-38   Lines in quotation marks are taken from a manual on how to apply for a grant from the U.S. Department of Justice.

p. 41   Italicized lines are taken from a wall in the American Visionary Art Museum in Baltimore, MD.

p. 60   The italicized line was lifted from graffiti since destroyed by D.C.'s "Clean City Initiative."

p. 63   Various lines are spliced from a letter-to-the-editor from a soldier in an unknown war published in an unknown newspaper.

p. 81   Victoria California Claflin was the first woman nominated for U.S. President. In 1872, she ran against Ulysses S. Grant on the ticket of the Equal Rights Party, well before women had the right to vote in the U.S. During her campaign, she was called a prostitute and lesbian and evicted from her home. She spent election day in jail after being arrested for sending literature that the U.S. government considered "obscene" through the mail. Incidentally, the newspaper she owned was the first to publish the *Communist Manifesto* in English. The Equal Rights Party's campaign song included the following lines:

> *Yes! Victoria we've selected*
> *For our chosen head.*
> *With Fred Douglass on the ticket*
> *We will raise the dead.*

A E R I A L / E D G E

Integrity & Dramatic Life, Anselm Berrigan, $10

They Beat Me Over the Head with a Sack, Anselm Berrigan, $4

Zero Star Hotel, Anselm Berrigan, forthcoming fall 2001

Comp., Kevin Davies, $12.

the julia set, Jean Donnelly, $4

Marijuana Softdrink, Buck Downs, $11

Metropolis 16–20, Rob Fitterman, $5

Dovecote, Heather Fuller, $10

perhaps this is a rescue fantasy, Heather Fuller, $10

Sight, Lyn Hejinian and Leslie Scalapino, $12

Late July, Gretchen Johnsen, $3

Stepping Razor, A. L. Nielson, $9

Ace, Tom Raworth, $10

Errata 5uite, Joan Retallack, $12

Dogs, Phyllis Rosenzweig, $5

Aerial 9: Bruce Andrews, Rod Smith, ed., $15

Aerial 8: Barrett Watten, $16

Aerial6/7 featuring John Cage, $15

Crow, Leslie Bumstead & Rod Smith, ed., $6

On your Knees, Citizen: A Collection of "Prayers" for the "Public" [Schools], Rod Smith, Lee Ann Brown, and Mark Wallace, eds., $6

Cusps, Chris Stroffolino, $2.50

Nothing Happened and Besides I Wasn't There, Mark Wallace, $9.50

Orders to: AERIAL/EDGE
             P.O. Box 25642
             Washington DC 20007

Add $1 postage for individual titles. Two or more titles postpaid.

W W W . A E R I A L E D G E . C O M